AF261123

WALTON WELL
CULTURE ART POETRY FICTION SOCIAL JUSTICE
PRESS

RUINED BEAUTY

ALSO BY MICHELLE BITTING

Nightmares & Miracles

Broken Kingdom

The Couple Who Fell to Earth

Notes to the Beloved

Good Friday Kiss

RUINED BEAUTY

Michelle Bitting

WALTON WELL PRESS
Los Angeles Oxford

Front Cover Art: *The Ecstasy of Saint Teresa* by Gian Lorenzo Bernini, c. 1647–1652.
Back Cover Art: The Relic of the Hand of St. Teresa of Avila.

Cover Design & Typesetting: ash good

Published by Walton Well Press
Los Angeles | Oxford
Editor: Theresia de Vroom

Paperback ISBN: 978-1-964295-15-2
Library of Congress Control Number: 2026909573

WALTONWELLPRESS.COM

for my students

Introduction

The cover of this book depicts a portion of the sculpture of the ecstasy of Saint Teresa of Ávila by Gian Lorenzo Bernini that resides in Cornaro Chapel of the church of Santa Maria della Vittoria in Rome. The sculpture is a depiction of the Roman Catholic saint (1515–1582). Bernini made the piece between 1647–1652. He came under intense scrutiny for the erotic depiction of the saint but argued, successfully, that he only depicted her own words. As she says:

> I saw in his hand a long spear of gold, and at the iron's point there seemed to be a little fire. He appeared to me to be thrusting it at times into my heart, and to pierce my very entrails; when he drew it out, he seemed to draw them out also, and to leave me all on fire with a great love of God. The pain was so great, that it made me moan; and yet so surpassing was the sweetness of this excessive pain, that I could not wish to be rid of it. The soul is satisfied now with nothing less than God. The pain is not bodily, but spiritual, though the body has its share in it. It is a caressing of love so sweet which now takes place between the soul and God, that I pray God of His goodness to make him experience it who may think that I am lying.

In Teresa's time women had no option but to marry and live domestic lives but they also had the choice of entering the convent where they could read and study and avoid that life. St. Teresa chose the latter. In the sixteenth century (and before) women were strictly forbidden to write on anything Biblical—so many turned to their own mystic and erotic fantasies of a relationship with Jesus or God—they were mystics—telling examples of "Ruined Beauty," the Anima—or female soul exposed.

As Michelle Bitting writes in her first poem of this collection:

Sudden

is the fire
like a wolf at a live heart

So many things
seem filled with intent

to be lost
but the only lasting truth is change

and if you had a limitless

life
it would be a real problem

Still

On the back cover is the reliquary hand of St. Teresa, which was cut off at her death and encased. It is an object of Catholic worship but in the end, it is the hand of a writer.

—*Theresia de Vroom*
Editor & Publisher, Walton Well Press

Poems

SUDDEN

THE PLAY

PRAYER MEETING

This struggle is sweeter than a life without dignity.
—Hanif Abdurraqib

These fragments I have shored against my ruins.
—Joan Didion

Everything ends with flowers.
—Helene Cixous

SUDDEN

Sudden

is the fire
like a wolf at a live heart

So many things
seem filled with intent

to be lost
but the only lasting truth is change

and if you had a limitless

life
it would be a real problem

Still

I wanted to come home
transformed

and be surprised
by the flickering

in our radically impermanent
robes

rain-soaked
and ringed with succulents

around
a tiled patio

where you'd put up the fairy lights

The mysterious nature of it—

all our rooms
all our ash

now a form
in emptiness
to visit

Life
as it really is

The inconsolable losses

The molten
heart

The Clearing

~ Los Angeles, after the January 7th fires

Funny to think how new I felt coming out of class that day,
Flush from the ballet rigors, sweating down the sidewalk—
A manzanita in bloom ready to begin again. I looked to the sky,
To the speaking gull passing, and beyond her an alien
Billowing mouth of dun and charcoal signs. I am remembering
This while fumbling to clasp a bronze bracelet given to me
After because everything was lost, of course, the ungrace
Of this catastrophic state I lean into, searching the singed box
Found in the smoking ruins, sifting for recipes, for favorites
Of ancestors where conversation flows more freely with
The dead. All that I dream, more familiar since flames
Leveled our former life, the taste of newfound nothingness
Rendered sharper by bones, sinew, and cherry port—it rocks me
Gently, this bracing tonic poured over the lot. We visited it
Last night. I watched you walk across like an astronaut sinking
Six feet into ashen muck. *I'm walking on the roof!* you cried,
Disappearing into morbid glitter, into satin aftermath—moonglow
Sifted over every beautiful thing, a lunar reduction. *It looks like*
Sunlit snow, said Buzz Aldrin when he first touched boot soles
To it. *Your pupils close down,* he said. Like layers
Of our lives contracting, we forget what has been, the record
Of the earth. I thought *Sometimes the sky's too bright,* then
Everything upside down turns black. *How can the moon be shining*
If we are standing on it? I asked you, my underworld husband,

My confection. Let's concentrate on where we are now—
Our cake of ambient people falling through rooms, through years
Collapsed to one luminous moment. I see you in the house,
There in our antique bed, your head between my legs
In the drowsy hours, our children chasing the dog,
Laughing at cartoons wrapped in Saturday morning
And blankets woven by aunties. Now I'm stirring
A kettle of Coq au Vin in my best blue overalls.
The hair at our temples glints of spare gray.
Now I'm watching you pull a cake
From the oven, the steaming gold dome
Of sherry and nutmeg batter—it sweetens
The rafters worn bare by love and rage.
In the end we found a magnificent desolation
And our way to see the stars through wars,
Through family demons and orbiting fires
The world performs around us on a horizon clearly
Curving away like a smile in an unknown language.

Manger, Emptied

We'd have no son for navigating midnight
Though I saw the shepherds slogging through red dust,
With palm trees sighing through green stars above.

This was in Los Angeles where the active site
Featured a bereft crèche, no babe front and center.
Stolen, we'd have no son for navigating midnight.

Everyone was somewhere else divining treasure to rub
Or holding for the light to reflect celebrated toes
With palm trees sighing through green stars above.

My mind's brittle ghosts threw down like dice
Among tossed-out hay, brash as gold.
Stolen, I'd have no sun to navigate midnight—

Or nest of foraged threads to rest my soul's bruised dove.
The heart that wants to rise and walk from its cage
With palm trees sighing through green stars above.

And of those playing it safe, who never speak up or fight,
While birds and branches scream a final *rubedo?*
Stolen, our sun planned for navigating midnight.

Before horizons bend and my brain's undone,
My cup will runneth over a melancholy rain
As palm trees sigh through green stars above.

Crib, trough, sleigh, coffin, where's unconditional love?
Manger meaning *mangier,* from Old French, meaning devoured.
Stolen, without a sound, now we navigate midnight
While palm trees sigh through green stars above.

Winter Reckoning

she said if you are new to this
dying, we will stand

at the gate together
beckoning back light

and the yule unfolding
its shadow

burning secrets
in the portal

my brother is in there
at a table with guests

hunched over roast
rosemary and silver

he was trying to say something
to make us laugh

but his switches all froze
his lamp already caught

in the under dark below
a slippery stitch

an abandoned cart
on an iced-over road

the homemade sweater
of holidays unraveling

we neglected to catch it
loss is never learned

always new but dimmer now
in the frigid hours

where skin and bones lift off
the raw meat of memory

awake as worms
tucked in snow

it stings to touch it
time's open basket

our merriment and tinsel
and a solstice moon

I step into
blank as a wound

as a bridge of silence
whatever drove him

it's day for night now
there is no other way

she said
at the gate of winter

I have seen birth
and death I said

I thought
they were different

Stable Epiphany

You wonder about unconditional love, if you're even capable, the grace of a baby left on the border of night and day, smallest voice in the void, in a dark world divided. Of have-nots humming another's hymns deemed gospel. And coming in from the cold. The book and a baby forced to read it back when. Pages sewn in blue to an imaginary womb. You take. You eat. You chew it all and wonder how in the endless loop of inns you're from: *Behold, I stand at the door and knock...* wasn't there always room for one more?

MEMORIAL

Now they're figuring out my brother's service.
It's a question of strict liturgy.

His love for Steely Dan another kind of liturgy.
Under the clergyman's collar one detects a faint rash.

A funeral playlist posted on Facebook augurs acting rash.
My mother took his model airplanes to the thrift shop after.

But who wants a broken anything after
Its tail's been clipped, its body gashed and blown

Windowless? A toy or gun or throat's trumpet blown.
I wish it were different.

Wings of rope, liquor, bullets—all the different
Flight plans a heart charts behind your back.

Once a thing's done there's no turning back.
Now they're figuring out my brother's service.

Boxing Day

My brothers are ghosts outside my house of words. They call me in to survey our shredded spoils. Father's fire blazes as cinders waft up the chimney. We learned to burn what wrapped treasure inside. *Wait*, I cry, *we should save this!* But Father tosses another box on the fire. Mother rushes in with instruments to accompany our burning cells. We play and watch black flames dance. So much heat and paper. And my brothers are ghosts outside the house of words. I dance inside with flames and watch my fires blaze. Then I waft up the chimney.

A Daughter Contemplates

How strokes and seizures have put him in the hospital again.
We come to say hello. He's eating chicken in a chair:

parmigiana, salad, ranch dressing and a roll. *Better than*
yesterday says the nurse when his mind was on

a boat, somewhere in San Diego, yanking tubes,
the strapped-on oxygen. Arm restraints. He who

never held back, he who stomped *I am the King!*
around the house—his throne front and center. After all

the chaos, here is his final crown: an EEG meter—the heady
Zeus bolts—everything under fire. I could object

how old age and infirmity so mercifully erase the past
in a white room where his face—so genuinely sweet,

so delighted to see me—as if my little boy, as if.
What is this all about? My mother at the window

repeating doctor reports, struggling to get it straight,
to comb it through her own weary folds. Half a century

he marched us, the spoils doled, the strict conditions—
captives and our promise of allegiance—my brothers not able to

make it, buried out there in ghost country. The quality
of mercy grows strained. His wife, his perennial sun,

sits confused, not knowing if rising or setting, a waning
orb. Hands grasp keys but can't hold where they go—

locked in a crib if it comes to it. They don't believe
I won't bolt, *silly*, so long ago I left but *look* how the machine

beeps on. He finishes his sorbet, the hospital tray I've
placed outside, needing to head home. He moves to stand,

thinking he's going with me, forgetting the nightie, the tube
sucking waste between his legs. Alarms will go off, the nurses

come running if he tries. He looks to me, hoping for
reprieve, and for a moment I love him mistaking me.

Whoever it is he believes I am.

Maybe Red Devils Run from My Heart

~ *after Stephen Crane*

The Pope held the hand of a child with Down Syndrome,
continuing his grand but humble mass at the Vatican altar

undisturbed after she burst through the crowd to be near him.
A barrier of police broken. On his deathbed: *Just bury me in a yard*

said the Pope—a simple plaque, my winnowed name. Well, *bravo*,
I thought, sick to death of the legacy parade that really means

people aren't okay with their mortality coming. I think of my mother
in a fitted dress of embroidered Chinese satin, at the stove in the old

mid-century A-frame, her hand delicate around the spoon, stirring
a pale pot of thickening béchamel. Her face perfectly made up—

movie star material she was, but the only acting she did
was to make everyone think she was really that happy. Now

she is old and calls me late at night slinging her grievances—
who is the child now? I'm nowhere near as nice as that Pope

and I lack heart to do more than long ago I learned—break lines and bolt
for what I need—a holiness that holds me still to this red and wicked life.

THE PLAY

The Play

My daughter was three and refused
to wear clothes. Naked on the living
room floor, she'd demand another round
of her favorite game, *Pretty Pretty Princess*,
then move the plastic rainbow markers
about the board—however, wherever
she pleased. Hair and legs wild, carefree,
splayed. She hated to lose and broke what
rules she had to while we laughed, astonished
at such nerve. Years later, she became a he,
and did what he had to, moving the markers
around wherever, however he needed,
winning the crown, himself, in the end.
Some rules are prettier, broken.

My Son Sleeps Off the Chemo While Another City's Under Siege

And I want to go back to the moment before.
The bombs fell. To glass on shelves rattling dust.
I want to go back to children with hands
raised and clasped in a singing game, in a circle
like a bell with laughter sparking light as it orbits
a yard or a body or a cupboard or a building's spontaneous
tomb. *The violin darkens then rises as smoke.* I want
the just before, the younger ones in pink and chartreuse
leggings, in striped and daisied jerseys, tilting their faces
to the complicated moons of older girls beaming
back at them, to heads circled in silk and signaling worry,
the spade of memory already driven deep into a sky of graves
where the killing aim is true as blood speeding through
the linked fingers of youth or my child's flesh-made hands.
Or a song humming along a warm mouth one minute then not.
As when the sky's indigo rivers mimic skin, disappearing inside
two palms touching at a place where the fortune teller peers,
tracking lines like tilled maps of human stars. Where is the angel
to predict what a path might take? I want to go back to the
moment before the bomb fell. When you told me about shadows,
about baby clusters like new fern heads in your chest,
ready to unfurl, the cells dividing, poised to drop. And after,
what it would come to, the chemical gold, the toxic terror we'd

deploy to stop them. How it's here that everything goes murky, goes to boiling black eclipse. And I keep wondering where the arms are for wrapping time, for keeping death swaddled tight. A stillborn thing to be flung from high and far off where no wings, no singing, no teeming innocent life could ever be expected—could ever be left—to break its fall.

Storm Drain

I am thinking about
how long it takes
the rain to find
a California window
the monumental glass
and unswept mine
of a ghost hotel
where
perched on a couch
five flights up, I'm
a struck kite
a wet mind
wading the muck
above time
and fallen water
along a Hollywood street
its dirty glittering
mirrors
choked with dead branches

Ode to My Son's Birthmark

Stork bite, angel kiss, salmon patch
of blush epidermis, pink palm print
pressed to the back of your head
& hidden until you merged
with the light outside my insides,
summer flooding the hospital room
in the city of Saint Monica, patron
of mothers & famous for cheering
son Augustine along his fraught
illustrious path & isn't the world
just like that? Mothers versus Death
since forever as we've followed it
in history books & life
& certainly since you arrived
on this planet so breathtakingly
artful in its design on evils
& delights, on miracles & mayhem
& shame on us & on me
forgetting your skull cap's masterpiece,
the field of Rorschach strawberry
where I'd plant my lips so often,
letting your follicle fragrance
fill me, a grace-given thing,
this infant essence, fecund
& flesh-scented, the bread
of stars if they could exhale
like animals, like the breath

of heaven, really, then…the unseen
illness, the taking of pictures,
the requisite shearing of locks
grown long in your young
adulthood—I saw it—the good
friends flying in with their weed
& spirits, their laughter
& raucous playlists, the ceremony
of love your goofy lot performed,
first braiding then snipping
then shaving your head to its
nubby minimum so the chemo
could not get there first,
that fucking devil we'd bless
& curse as it snaked its orange
burn around your body
in the coming weeks & months
& how the shearing brought the mark
into view, the rouge kiss of a long-lost
lover peeking through your homemade
beanie knit by a family friend
from the church we don't visit
anymore, not even on holidays
or to pray in pews under stained glass
where divinity streams through—Oh,

you brave & worthy knight,
your body a cathedral, your bones,
holy relics humming the hymns
of coming health & weren't we
the ones back when, always first
to the healing rail, our heads bowed
to receive the woo-woo spirit where
most were too proud
or embarrassed to kneel or believe
but we knew that *the things worth*
knowing are not the things we know
& when *God is gone* it means
church is everywhere & water
might turn to wine & stones to gold
& the greatest moment in the service
was when everything stopped
& the veil of words dropped
like a curtain of hair falling
& the people turned to touch
each other, saying *Peace be with you*
& *Also with you*, their trembling
hands a little like newborn
roses opening to morning
after the shadow of night has passed

Pieces of the Past

Rise up from the rubble, back from when I was convinced there wasn't anyone who'd want a skinny forlorn fool like me draped in black chiffon like Masha from the 19th century play about narcissists and suicides. Can you imagine if I'd stayed home that night in mourning for my life? To get nothing worth nourishing out of the lonely spell of sitting by yourself in a dark room staring into the faulty fire escape of a double bourbon, well, you'll drown trying, my dear, you'll drown—just another tragic character from an old tale by a Russian poet. In other words, thank gods I went to the party and made a pact with you, a raft with you, made our two pups with you, which made the four of us bobbing out here in the muddle of this poem which is the middle of an ocean I don't ever want to get out of.

Disaster Fat

No way not to pack the extra pounds back on. Grief dictated we swallow copious sugar, flour, cream—comfort foods passed daily our direction. Confounding, but hardly brutal, our bad luck, compared to others, the pounded world. Look how safe we stayed! Wrapped in an obesity of kindness. Delivered in corpulent forms: in puddings, steaks, posh lamps and stuffed pleather chairs. In hand-stitched quilts flush with every succulent color, shrouding the scorch, the insurance claim blaze. Flung to our doorstep? Not bombs but bags of donated clothes. Each friend, each heavenly body making the scars of all that burned fade from our lot's smoked history. *Forests may be gorgeous, but there's nothing more alive than a tree that learns to grow in a cemetery.* If, that is, there's love. Even a seed.

~ with a line by Andrea Gibson

Late Afternoon

Beyond the limits
of longing
a patchwork
of shadows and light
because winter
and a window
and the other side of the pane
a frozen sun
where leaves tremble
dropping their dappled
display
what you have been
you have
the potential to become
again, I said
I want to travel the world
he said
imagining the country
a French chateau
a girl in a room
thick with books
thick as a forest
lullaby
an alchemy

of thoughts
warming his cheeks
to Rosicrucian
and a fire
inside the walls
its burning message
that says— *thou art God*

Spicer's Radar

~ after Jack Spicer after Marianne Moore

In that moment no one exactly knows the direction the cloud swims or how my face looks to the mountain's eye going on a hungry journey. First, a fat heart unburies itself. Then, this handful of granola sanded with turmeric reminds me of gold. Passing as if it were sun. Go ahead. I couldn't make out the shine of what you were saying anyway. When we murmur emotions, which stream do we demure? Our fears help us admire every last drop of ocean. It starts off as tactic but then we're overwhelmed. The cloud's noise. Bereaved beds. The humpbacked mountain pushing deep the sand's edge. The eye jealous of whatever moves.

Ruined Beauty

I decided to continue on   best I can   no one wants to see
an entire town   go up in flames   the list of objects
described to friends   sounds like a poem   someone said
it took all night   to pull it to ashes   what remains of our lot
among trees left smoking   in their specter jackets   the chimney stacks
of branded bricks   shadow soldiers   keeping watch   over their ravaged
hamlets   the carcass-strewn fields   including my 1957   Royal Quiet Deluxe
typewriter   a Sci-Fi Festival bumper sticker   the kids slapped to the old metal
mailbox   twenty years ago   its white mouth   unhinged and hanging open
as if aghast   at the storm's   obscene delivery   our former yard's
stone Buddha   our angel   and St. Francis figure   his sculpted robes
cast in soot   as if in mourning for wild animals   caught in the blaze
as they fled the burning hills   the tattered scrap   of our son's PRIDE flag
flapping against the porch swing's frame   the next morning   I won't exhaust you
with my litany of loss   only pause to confess   how little I actually care
to cling to our life before   or objects held dear   in my mind's newly minted eye
my fetal view thrust through   an avalanche of blood and cinder   afterbirth
my alien landing   and unplanned arrival   on an inverted Earth   the good bad
and ugly packed   into time's combustible rooms   can you forgive me?
my refusal to weep forever   choking on dirt   on toxic dust   the sand
of hours   slipping through glass   the father's toppled citadel
my bones dank   in their rainy aftermath   but dancing just the same
down a path to raw wonder   to curtains rising   on a brand-new art?

I'm told the Eiffel Tower   gets repainted   every seven years
since completion   in the 19th century   on my honeymoon   I got halfway

up the hydraulic elevator   and had a minor breakdown   suddenly
claustrophobic   in the crowded cab   with my husband   atop a foreign city
famous for non-stop sparkle   that flows all hours   and I couldn't stop
sweating   through my silk   it was shameful   how I screamed to   *Let me
off!   S'il vous plait!*   the paint job gets repeated   more often now
everything quicker and more urgent   for the nowhere   we think we're
getting to   complicit with the rate   of things worn down   faster than we
can fix them   I tear myself   and bolt from any cage   at Olympic speed
and by the way   they cloaked the Eiffel Tower   in coats of gold   for the '24
Olympics   the goal   my gall   after thirty years   trapped   living near the sea
where my house   expired   I rose like a red bird   above a ravaged city   now I could fly
in my mind   anywhere   to imagined Parisian terrain   of edible underpants even
of Beaux Arts and baguettes   matcha macarons   Bach at Saint Chapelle
or the absurd grandeur   of mirrored halls   and fabricated cottages   for
the dirty-pawed pugs   of Antoinette   or a miniature Notre Dame   made from
wickedly plush chocolate   in the Montmartre shop   near Sacre Coeur   where my son
and I once lit candles   to dead uncles   and our gone dog Charlie   enough novenas
to guide us down   whatever bleak path   comes next   the circling clockwork
of pain   as Pessoa once put it   the day's dimmed forest   must we go there ever again?
the night the French cathedral   erupted in flame   it was a smoldering lattice
in the attic's wooden forêt   that undid it   unlike my town   the hidden sparks
of New Year's rockets   delinquent males   left festering for days   embers and wind
awakening the underbrush   casting a spell   sprung like a cat   to consume the privileged
town whole   that believed itself immune   how many times   did I curse that place
shielding my spirit   soldiering on as mother   lover, teacher, friend?   my armor tempered

like Joan on her road to Rouen? three times they tried to burn her heretic's heart
finally succeeding finally tossing its ashen husk to the Seine that fistful
of ruined beauty a sifted testament to the dark art of what gets writ on water
a someday salvation I tremble to think on now love the shuddering monster
the surviving essential risen within and made from worms and elves from skillets
carvings shelves you know *her kind* forgive me, Lord the sin of speaking
through fire the heat in my hands these lantern fingers burning at the gate
of words my future sealed to all its fine horrors each letter a seed a cell
destroying itself to let greener wings unfurl blade and bough a witching cloud
unstaked and passing across radiant clocks the sun and moon keeping time keeping
watch over every heavenly minute and the unseen worlds inside ready to burn

PRAYER MEETING

Prayer Meeting

~ an ars poetica with a line by Terrance Hayes

I wanted to start with the orange light
and end with the lemon tree. The old
Ford was a lemon, and I wanted
the dashboard's flashing emergency
to dénouement into a poet's stately
haiku. Ripe fruit resting at the end
of a heavily winnowed branch. Looking
to be plucked or simply contemplated,
depending if you are here to appreciate
miracles or slice them open, drizzle
honey and suck the dueling notes
of sweet & sour until you're a fusion
of flavored smoke inside the beekeeper's
billow. I have been that unafraid and I have
welcomed the inspection of my hives.
How often they make no sense while
emitting a chemical order. The poem
as life as moment propped on a stem
of green nutrients unveiling its sting.
Pieces of puzzle made into keys
for unlocking bones of the inscrutable
self. Or hole in the mirror. Which is reason
to search my glove compartment

for a manual to fix anything. So we can
get somewhere. Pages rifled that connect
signs & sounds with a feeling inside
like a psalm *taking flight over the weeping fields*
where blackbirds are sleeping. A poem
the bible or muse open to interpretation. Scrip-
ture as invention that comes in handy say
my relatives from the cleave in the middle of
the country. A new view like a miracle they say
can happen. And I can agree
in the same way I know gods might appear
out of nowhere. Even this small flock
of neon green parrots flashing early
along winter skies, boisterous & flamboyant
as emerald matadors shaking sequined
sleeves across an eternity of air. Or the wet
& trembling jewels of late November rain.
Ecstasy and a man surprising himself naked
& wild leaping from the tub where the gold
of unknowing is more precious than mineral
value or what's suppressed in the weighing.
After your theatrical set, the audience
erupting. How it was then that the Volta
made her dramatic essence known inside
a buzzing cacophony of praise & fluster.

Noise falling away like ready lemons from
a limb. Time stopping as when a haiku breathes
or spreads its momentary feathers. How
your face pivoted my direction inside
the adoring cloud like a bird or knife
in flight looking to land and my warning
lights flushed red. My comportments opened.
Instruction pages laying themselves bare, holy
as apparitions. In the end, it was the
beginning, and the good word was you
out of nowhere turning to ask *Is there somewhere*
I'm supposed to be? And me not hesitating
to answer *Where is it you'd like to go?*

Lost in the Disco Ball

No reason to fear the last or open
call. When Twyla picked me to dance
back in the 90's, I died.
It was heaven
collapsing in the doorway
after the sweaty all-day
audition. The film
I got cast to dance in
died despite Prince's
soundtrack and his *party like*
it's 1999 spirit. Pretty soon,
I'll fly to London
with my reddest, sleep-
deprived eyes. In the past,
I'd call in sick if even
the wind upset my son.
Autism's airier elements
blasting every sense
and direction. Does love
last a lifetime? I can tell you
sorry-ass is an overused expression
but Lang's *Metropolis*
inspired a whole new chapter
of my novel. Like Rome,
I'm on fire. In a secret cupboard

behind the liquor cabinet
of my childhood home. Un-
stoppable. I can live
with less but not without
art. Also, I'm not always
good and it's okay.
I wish there was a way
one of my brothers was still alive.
In the next chapter
of my novel, I'll look
for them in London
sweating like dogs
in need of rescue.
While I try
not to collapse in a doorway
watching them. Their sorry asses
dancing in the wind.

Ode on a Line by Marie Howe

~ If I got on my knees, might I lift my life as a turtle carries her home?

And what would I see there
beneath the mud
of flooded deserts, of dirty
runes and pages pressed with dust
to passing hours? So long I looked
for severed diadems, meaning
I really was obsessed—
a child hunting the hills
haunting my house, rocks with lapidary
yolks found secreted, lithic
eggs I was told when cleaved
revealed a violent shimmering.

I wanted it more than gold, more
than lapis, quartz or the Tongvan
honed obsidian, pitch
arrows if you're lucky
to recover anything intact—the boys
enthralled with weaponry and tools.
As I was, a fortshaper, a brush brute
clearing the past in service of rooms
for burnt imaginings, bushels
of them, my floors wept clean—no
leaves or poison left—just talking mats
of welcoming spiders, yucca, sage.

Step on it I said, imagining palaces,
their crystal hiddenness, a granite
heart I can split and lift
above like Atlas. I'm on my knees
dissolving what remains now—
stones to glitter, to semiprecious
pools, soft and luminous
as water, as the moons of my
children's faces, humorous
as when I squeezed
their slippery eggs into the earth
under this shell and its crumbling
cosmos, under worlds where I write this,
where I will bury myself, singing.

Twyla

As in Tharp, as in star, as in choreo
Queen of the spotlit postmodern stage,
Not to be mistaken with Thorpe, legendary
Athlete from Oklahoma's Sac & Fox Nation
& first Native American to win gold
At the 1912 Olympics, yet in terms
Of sheer virtuosity, you could call them
Birds of a feather firing the air
With flight out of the starting block,
Their aerodynamic feats, raw grace
& vigorous art that makes the nest
Of a young girl's mind hatch dreams
Of marrying those bodies in motion—to flex
& vault & leap alongside them—Mercury's
Javelin cinched to arches as they sprint
From Delphi to Athens, from Paris to L.A.,
The torch held historically aloft while
The breath of life thrums on, heat & drum
Of an ignited heart, and what is the heart
But a muscle of need, of music supreme—
Its own little Catherine Wheel striking sparks
Around the blood's spectacle tributaries—heart
Like a circus barker calling us to the tent
So we can cheer the games as one—heart
That pulses, cartwheels & sometimes plummets,

Robbed of its medals, its good shoes & glory
Falling in its prime only to get up again
Like I once saw Twyla do before a Philly audience,
Pirouetting out of the glitch like it was nothing
But candle flicker, her quicksilver steps, her signature
Recovery—flash of tumble, kick & high jump—
The iconoclast hips turned out & then in against
Tradition—dance so speedy, sensual—I thought
C'est n'est pas possible, mon Dieu! Quite bewitching
If you mean wicked unconventional as all
Great magicians are, shocking us to the future—well,
Who wouldn't bare their chest? The flesh curtain
Parted, red organ plucked for a taste of rare fire?
To steal it is pure gold as any artist knows
And we are only human, and I have seen art stop time—
Fear's watch smashed senseless on my ticking wrist
In service of lightning on stage, on the track, in the gym
Of audacity—skill & endurance—the body a disciple
Searching for truth in the upper room of desire
& what divinity burns unfettered there—hearth of Hestia,
Hand of Prometheus, the flare of hope defying gravity,
Tyranny, defeat—*Creativity is an act of defiance*
Tharp once stated—the sport of making, a poetry
In motion—the constellating stars that Jim Thorpe,
Born *Wa-Tho-Huk,* meaning *Bright Path*

Must have seen when his running deeds
Were done & a string of silken wind
Crossed his chest, crossing the finish line,
The crowd of watchers rising
To witness it, feeling more alive,
Feeling like they, too, were flying.

Self Portrait with Spit-Up Hades

At times I've danced
so hard, even the unseeing
gods demanded I stop,
you know,
running away with it
like that, vomiting away
with it like that. I remember
death is not bad
for the one who dies.
I remember
how language drifts
down on us
in heavy feathers—
an over pour of words
of overripe fruit
from the attic of fathers,
we clip
and scissor
with our sharpest wings
and a prayer
for rarer weather. Why
did I dive here
when I know the mirror
knows better? Now I'm
the lady having a hair day,
her bad head wedged
in the down below

dream, the gutter
glittered,
a black diamond lake
tasting of apricot
& lassi. When my
tongue flies apart,
I fight its raw speed
and swallow trickling
light
through warm June
rain. When coyotes
come circling
in dark of night,
I promise
not to feed them
the spirit sleeve
fastened at my wrist
with living moss. So no
beast sniffs out
my still wet wounds—
a little red and scabby,
a little animal
around the edges where
I'm still hunting enough
sun
to make oblivion a scar.

Rumpus Room

Here I will enact my good and evil
I will curse the dead and the living
The living mostly
I will also get down
Naked on all fours
And let my beloved take me
Our knees sinking deeper
Into the faux fur rug
About the ones I curse
I'll say
They can be so nice
Ask anyone at their church
But what about the vitriol?
Late at night
Spit across wires and lines
Lumps of hidden spite
Of aging baggage lugged
Are camels nocturnal?
I saw one once
Bathing in the Arabian Sea
It was beautiful
Her rummaging around the waves
The water cool and cradling her
We must avoid a poison heart
We must fight for time in the rumpus

Where the wild things go
To sail and stomp away
And gnash their teeth
They are not afraid to cry
Some animals spit when they're afraid
Things like death
The room where we're sent with no dinner
I should care more, I know
I should be more forgiving
They'll be gone soon enough
While my Turkish lamp glows green
The pillows are soft
And I've got Nina Simone
On my retro Victrola
It spins a little slow
So she's sounding extra sorrowful
I'm letting her swallow me
Like quicksand
Like the sea
Like a beautiful beast
Rolling in waves
Casting a spell
Its good wickedness
Its good song

I want it to last
My beloved bending
And kneeling again
And again for me
It will all be over soon enough

I Get You, Norma Desmond

Keats called it Negative Capability, Lorca called it Duende.
That's my religion if I have one. ~ Diane Seuss

Though I'll never be interested in orchestrating
funerals for satin-clad chimps, or murdering
studly young screenwriters hired to revive my
Hollywood career. My fall from brilliance to has-
been. Nothing wrong with being 50 unless you're
set on 25 & unbecoming formaldehyde fantasies.
And while I do dig wearing dark glasses any hour
of the day & even indoors, I don't care for guns
or burying simian buddies in empty rat-pocked
pools, or, conversely, watching my chums float
face down & bullet-riddled when blue water
ripples through them. You get the picture. Easy on
the leopard skin, Honey. A pill box hat & peacock
feather, a smattering of paw-printed undies
suffices. Way too dramatic seeing pelt stitched
into every turban, robe, & tapestry—the sleek
upholstered corners of my convertible
Isotta Fraschini. Animal & blood lusty. Perpetual
swaddling in predatory branding—who needs it?
Standing here where

                    the cross fade happens. Where
the shot dissolves & screen splits. Roads diverging

in the forest of immortality. Who needs to breathe
forever? The great Gloria Swanson—doppelgänger
to Desmond, but never so delusional, said it
best: *Life and death. They are somehow sweetly*
and beautifully mixed, and I don't know how. Such
mystery bringing us, Reader, to Seuss's epigraph
& some point this poem is floating around
like a body in a swimming pool or fire reflected
in the eyes of an ape gazing into a hearth's dying
blaze in a lonely star's boudoir. Or the cloud
& palm-tufted heavens rushing above us
motoring along this Bel-Air boulevard
in our posh, imported car. The postcard sunset
& scent of almonds & orange blossoms, of moth
balls & tuberoses—intoxicating, disturbing
as the thousand ways we might imagine Wilder's
protagonist or our own personal demise
on the pages of anyone's imagination. To believe
the world's forgotten you & love fades like
old lipstick, leaving you to languish under covers
with your taped & bandaged wrists. To play with
pills & 80 proof booze or a lengthy, finite dive
off the long face of a building. Well, who hasn't
diddled death even a little? Where Keats & Lorca

were concerned, negative & capable link hands—
twinning, inseparable. An up and down carousel
of white & raven horses & all the weird gray noise
in between. *Those dark sounds are the mystery, the roots
that cling to the mire we all know, and all ignore,* Lorca said.
Deranged & broken souls sewn with duende,

we suspect, is why. In college I was cast as
Death in Euripides' play about a tortured
spouse who must surrender his life to the
underworld should he wish to see his wife
again. I danced & skirted the edges of Berkeley's
monstrous Greek theater. I dressed in black
OshKosh overalls & had at it—twirling, miming,
winding my way through the audience & stadium
seats. A silent Salome-like pantomime. My mane
of bobbed blond curls whipping wind behind
me as I spun whimsical, fatal tableaus. Admetus
desperate to retrieve his beloved Alcestis wedded
to oblivion in the mosh pit below. Her morbid
journey, her finish halted when madman Heracles
descends in perfect deus ex machina to make it
all right again. Tragedy blighted. Life won. This
was 1982 and my director George House took his
cue from Fosse—*All That Jazz* a recent hit with

the sultry Jessica Lange playing angelic reaper.
An ultimate seduction. A fever dream desire &
no escape. Sex & Death at the rabbit hole's end.
George was rotund, loved opera, boys, chain-
smoking & bourbon. Also, professional wrestling
he'd watch for hours from his decadent bed
of vermillion caftans & gold embroidered
kimonos—otherwise naked in his low-lit, baubled
bedroom. I cleaned his house once a week when
I wasn't in class, rehearsal, or scoring drugs &
vintage clothing off Shattuck & Center. He was
a slob, a diva, a Norma Desmond in drag & I
loved him. Even the toilet bowl scum, rancid
fridge & sauce crusted stove I was forced to scrub.
The scuffed floors & laundry loads & liquor bottles.
I didn't mind. I just wish I'd been there when his
heart stopped & he toppled, alone, to his end—tabby
cats circling, meowing for their dinner. I would have
been there—his Max—his deus to descend or direct,
to worship or revive or sweep up. Long after
the reaching has stopped. Here's the thing. I'm ready
for my closeup. When it comes to life, when it
comes to art—once it starts—the reaching never
ends. All those beating, homo sapien hearts. All
those wonderful people out there in the dark.

Before Disappearing into the Fog

of dust & darkness
I remember spring in Los Angeles

near the coast
means fog and how

the chill can make morning
a confusion

a fog of minuets
in Mozart's notebooks

can't compete with it
the fog's true desire

this morning
a fugue infusion

for the piano
while I coax spring

from slices of cantaloupe
their ripe hips

a fog of juice
caught above my chin

a sticky chill
I shiver in

fog blankets the spring
we must embrace it

here near the sea
soaked in fog

where feathered radiance
streaks the sky

the heat of light
burning off grief

overnight
where the cream bursts

in a fog of bulbs
strolling the arms

of magnolia branches
an erotic alarm

the way the geese
above foggy lagoons

keep on erupting
their horns

a wing of music
that slaps the fog silly

lifting my despair
that will die

in a fog
meeting yours

our fog of dark notes
sprung like birds

we inter in the sky
before we're buried alive

The Grain of Gold Waving in the Sun

What better moment than now to praise the gardener, the dancing grin of her scythe clawing circles around time? Let no trouble decay heart: moth and rust we'll not abide. Nor thieves breaking in to steal this final sip: a drop of kindness keeping vigil over the cradle, the grail of day that breaks like glass with much to mourn. My eye is a lamp in my body. Still. Praise bounty. Praise bread, the wine, the crust, and fleeting kiss setting flame to tongue. That keeps us tilling—Love—that keeps us turning in the sun.

Acknowledgments

"Manger, Emptied" — *Cleaver Magazine*
"Winter Reckoning" — *Thrush*
"Stable Epiphany" — *100 Word Story*
"MEMORIAL" — *The National Poetry Review*
"Boxing Day" — *Postcard Literature*
"A Daughter Contemplates" — *Journal of Compressed Creative Arts*
"The Play" — *SWWIM*
"My Son Sleeps Off the Chemo While Another City's Under Siege"
— *ONE Jacar Press*
"Storm Drain" — *The Banyan Review*
"Ode to my Son's Birthmark" — *Poetry Society of New York / Milk Press*
"Pieces of the Past" — *Catamaran*
"Disaster Fat" — *Anacapa Review*
"Late Afternoon" — *One Art—A Journal of Poetry*
"Spicer's Radar" — *Heavy Feather Review*
"Ruined Beauty" — *The Ilanot Review*
"Prayer Meeting" — *The Missouri Review* (Poem of the Week)
"Lost in the Disco Ball" — *The Pedestal*
"Ode on a Line by Marie Howe" — *Elysium Review*
"Twyla" — Finalist, the 2024 DCA Paris/L.A. Olympiad Cultural Exchange
"Self Portrait with Spit-Up Hades" — *The Glacier*
"Rumpus Room" — *Action, Spectacle*
"I Get You, Norma Desmond" — *Gargoyle*
"The Grain of Gold Waving in the Sun" — *Terrain*
"MEMORIAL" was featured on *Verse Daily*, 2025
"The Clearing" won *The Banyan Review* Poetry Prize, 2025

Notes

"Sudden" "The Clearing" and "Ruined Beauty" were written in response to the Palisades— Eaton fires on January 7th, 2025. "Sudden" references lines by Anne Sexton, Octavia Butler, Elizabeth Bishop, and Thích Nhât Hanh's Heart Sutras. "The Clearing" ends on a line by Fernando Pessoa.

"Winter Reckoning" references T.S. Eliot's poem "The Journey of the Magi."

The line *Behold, I stand at the door and knock* in "Stable Epiphany" taken from *The Bible,* Book of Revelation, 3:20.

"Maybe Red Devils Run from my Heart" plays on a poem by Stephen Crane.

"The Play" inspired by Kim Addonizio and Emmet Abrams

In "My Son Sleeps Off the Chemo While Another City's Under Siege", the line *The violin darkens then rises as smoke* references Paul Celan's poem "Todesfuge."

"Storm Drain" inspired by Jack Spicer's poem "Psychoanalysis: An Elegy."

"Ode to my Son's Birthmark": *The things worth knowing are not the things we know & God is gone* taken from script lines in the series *Outer Range.*

"Pieces of the Past" references Anton Chekhov's *The Seagull* and Jack Spicer's poem "Any fool can get into an ocean."

"Late Afternoon" is for Thomas Farmer.

"Disaster Fat" includes a line by the poet Andrea Gibson.

"Ruined Beauty" references the great French martyr Jeanne D'Arc, poet John Keats's notable epitaph, and Anne Sexton's remarkable poem "Her Kind."

"Prayer Meeting" was inspired by Major Jackson and Myka Kielbon at *The Slowdown*.

"Twyla" was commissioned by the Los Angeles Cultural Affairs Department for the 2024 Paris/ Olympiad cultural exchange.

"I Get You, Norma Desmond" contains many visual, plot, and dialogue references to the 1950 film *Sunset Boulevard*, directed by Billy Wilder.

Biggest heart to Theresia, Gail, ash, Phil, Emmet, Eli, Lee, Major, my family, friends, and students.

ABOUT THE AUTHOR

Michelle Bitting is the author of five previous collections of poetry including *Good Friday Kiss*, winner of the inaugural De Novo First Book Award (C & R Press); *Notes to the Beloved*, which won the Sacramento Poetry Center Book Award (reissued by C & R Press); *The Couple Who Fell to Earth* (C & R Press); *Broken Kingdom*, winner of the 2018 Catamaran Poetry Prize, and *Nightmares & Miracles* (Two Sylvias Press, 2022), winner of the Wilder Prize. Her chapbook *Dummy Ventriloquist* launched in 2024 from C & R Press. Michelle is a Senior Lecturer in Creative Writing and Literature at Loyola Marymount University.

www.ingramcontent.com/pod-product-compliance
Lightning Source LLC
Chambersburg PA
CBHW050039040726
47599CB00015B/1751

* 9 7 8 1 9 6 4 2 9 5 1 5 2 *